Chef

This edition published by Scholastic Inc., 557 Broadway, New York, NY 10012, by arrangement with QEB Publishing, Inc., 3 Wrigley, Suite A, Irvine, CA 92618

www.qeb-publishing.com

Library of Congress Cataloging-in-Publication Data

Askew, Amanda.
   Chef / by Amanda Askew ; illustrated by Andrew Crowson.
      p. cm. -- (QEB people who help us)
   ISBN 978-1-59566-993-3 (hardcover)
   1. Cooks--Juvenile literature. 2. Cookery--Juvenile literature. I. Crowson, Andrew. II. Title.
   TX652.5.A75 2010
   641.5092--dc22

2009001988

ISBN: 978-1-59566-902-5

10 9 8 7 6 5 4 3 2 1

Printed and bound in China

Author Amanda Askew
Designer and Illustrator Andrew Crowson
Consultants Shirley Bickler and Tracey Dils

Publisher Steve Evans
Creative Director Zeta Davies
Managing Editor Amanda Askew

Words in bold are explained in the glossary on page 24.

People who help us

Chef

Amanda Askew
Andrew Crowson

QEB Publishing

Meet Rory. He's a chef. He cooks food for people at Rory's Diner.

Rory arrives at his **restaurant** at 9 o'clock in the morning. The kitchen workers are there to help him **prepare** the food for lunch.

First, Rory goes over the **menu**.

"Today, we'll cook leek and potato soup, lamb chops with mint gravy, and chocolate fudge cake."

6

"Josh, chop the vegetables for the soup. Alice, mix the chocolate cake. Greg, prepare the mint gravy and the mashed potato swirls."

Josh, Greg, and Alice start working.

Alice gets the "Chocolate Delight" recipe.

8

Josh starts to chop the leeks and peel the potatoes.

Greg picks fresh mint from the herb garden.

Alice starts to collect her **ingredients**.

"Oh, no! The refrigerator has broken down! All the food is ruined!" she shouts.

Rory rushes over to the fridge.

The milk, butter, and cheese can't be used. The stock for the gravy will have to be thrown away. The lamb chops will have to be replaced.

Rory calls Farmer John. "We've got an emergency. The refrigerator is broken. We need milk, butter, cheese, and lamb chops—they were today's special."

"I have everything except lamb chops. Will chicken be okay?"

"Yes, that's fine. I'll serve chicken with mushrooms instead," says Rory.

Farmer John delivers the new food.

Rory and the team work hard to get everything ready for lunchtime.

People start to arrive at the restaurant at 12 o'clock.

"Three chicken dishes to table 5 please, Freda," Rory says.

19

By 2 o'clock, most people are eating their desserts. Rory goes into the **dining area** to meet some of the customers. He likes to see that everyone is happy with their food.